Pooh and the Storm That Sparkled

Disney's
Winnie the Pooh First Readers

Pooh Gets Stuck
Bounce, Tigger, Bounce!
Pooh's Pumpkin
Rabbit Gets Lost
Pooh's Honey Tree
Happy Birthday, Eeyore!
Pooh's Best Friend
Tiggers Hate to Lose
The Giving Bear
Pooh's Easter Egg Hunt
Eeyore Finds Friends
Pooh's Hero Party
Pooh's Surprise Basket
Pooh and the Storm That Sparkled

DISNEY'S

A Winnie the Pooh First Reader

Pooh and the Storm That Sparkled

Adapted by Isabel Gaines

ILLUSTRATED BY Studio Orlando

DISNEY PRESS

NEW YORK

First Edition

1 3 5 7 9 10 8 6 4 2
This book is set in 18-point Goudy.

Library of Congress Catalog Card Number: 98-86648

ISBN: 0-7868-4313-6 (paperback)

For more Disney Press fun, visit www.DisneyBooks.com

Pooh and the Storm That Sparkled

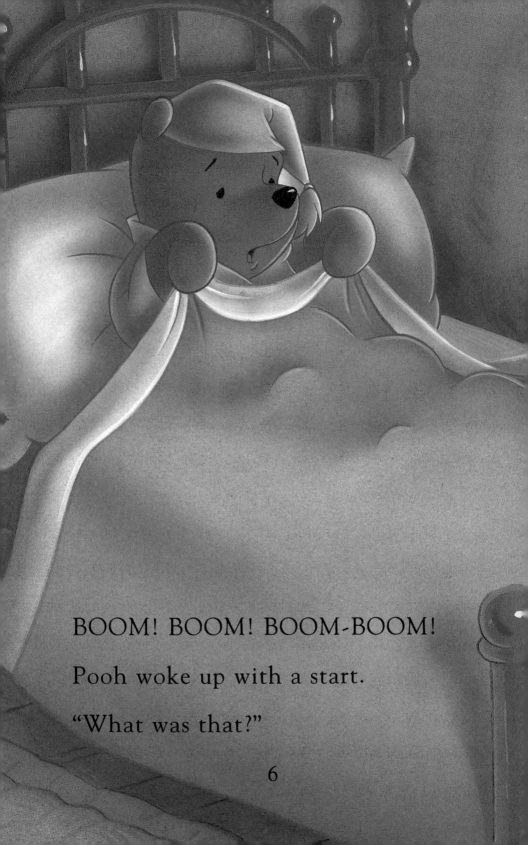

BOOM! BOOM! BOOM-BOOM!

Pooh woke up with a start.

"What was that?"

There was a knock

at the door.

"Who's there?" said Pooh.

"Pooh, help!" a voice cried.

"Is that you, Piglet?"

"Yes!" said Piglet.

Pooh opened the door.

"A heffalump is after me!"

said Piglet.

"Where is it?" said Pooh.

"I don't know," said Piglet.

"I can only hear it."

BOOM! BOOM-BOOM! BOOM!

"The heffalump!" said Piglet.

Pooh looked out the door.

"Look!" said Pooh. "A red

flash! Now a white flash!

And a blue one!"

11

"Piglet," Pooh said,

"I believe your heffalump

is not a heffalump.

12

"It is a very bad storm.
What we hear is thunder
and what we see is lightning."
"I have never seen lightning
in so many colors," said Piglet.

"The storm is behind
the Great Hill," said Pooh.
"Oh dear," said Piglet.
"The last storm
blew Owl's house down."

"We better warn the others,"

said Pooh. "I'll get my honeypots."

BOOM! BOOM! BOOM! BOOM!

"What was that?" asked Owl.

He looked out his window.

He saw Pooh and Piglet

at his door.

"Owl," said Pooh,

"a big storm is coming."

"Here's a pot of honey
for you," said Pooh,
"so that you don't have
to go out for more food."

"Thank you, Pooh," said Owl.

"Let's warn Rabbit," said Pooh.

"A bad storm?" said Rabbit.

He looked up in the sky.

"But there are no clouds."

RABBITS
HOUSE

"That's because the storm

is still far away," answered Owl.

"It is a very bad storm," said Pooh.

BOOM! BOOM! BOOM! BOOM!

"Hear the thunder?" said Piglet.

"Rabbit, here's a pot of honey,"
said Pooh, "so that you
don't have to go
out for more food."
"Thank you, Pooh," said Rabbit.

"We have to warn Tigger," said Pooh.

"Tigger is not home," said Rabbit.

"He went on a picnic

with Kanga, Roo,

and Christopher Robin."

"B-B-But they will be near trees!"
cried Piglet.

"Christopher Robin told me
never to be near a tree
in a lightning storm!"

"We must save them," said Pooh.

"They are on the Great Hill,"

said Rabbit.

"The Great Hill!" cried the others.

"That is where the storm is!"

said Pooh.

Pooh, Piglet, Owl, and Rabbit
climbed the Great Hill.

The BOOMS got louder and louder.

The lightning was red,

green, gold, and blue.

It was round and sparkly
and made pretty patterns in the sky.
"I w-w-wish Christopher Robin
was here," cried Piglet.

They were at the top

of the hill.

They stopped short.

"What kind of storm

is this?" asked Pooh.

Christopher Robin ran

up to them.

"Happy Fourth of July!

Come watch the fireworks with us."

"But, Christopher Robin,"
said Pooh, "we've come
to save you from the storm."

"Silly bear," said Christopher Robin.

"It's not a storm.

They are fireworks!

Come join us."

And that's what they did.

"Oooo," said Pooh.

"Aaahh," said Piglet.